Original title:
In the Embrace of Kindred Spirits

Copyright © 2024 Creative Arts Management OÜ
All rights reserved.

Author: Charles Whitfield
ISBN HARDBACK: 978-9916-94-334-2
ISBN PAPERBACK: 978-9916-94-335-9

**Whispers of Familiar Hearts**

Beneath the stars we share our snacks,
Jokes fly like boomerangs, no lack.
Chicken dance and silly hats,
Best friends in our fluffy spats.

With every giggle, we do collide,
Laughter's wave, it's quite the ride.
In our own world, we prance and twine,
Like kittens in a yarn-filled line.

## **Unity in Serendipity**

Stumbling on each other's toes,
A dance that only true friends know.
Two left feet in a right-foot game,
Together we're as wild as flames.

Chasing pigeons in the park,
Chit-chatting like we're a spark.
With silly hats and ice cream mess,
The day's become a pure success.

## **Bonds Woven in Moonlight**

Under the moon, we strut and sway,
Crickets chirp, join the ballet.
We're socked in sandals, quite the look,
Each laugh a giggle in the book.

With hidden secrets and silly dreams,
Making potions with wild schemes.
The night glows bright with cheeky cheer,
Together always, never fear.

## **Souls Entwined in Laughter**

Tickle fights and midnight chats,
Creating chaos like bumbling bats.
We paint the town with silly grace,
In our little, happy place.

With pranks that dance on every street,
Every moment feels like a treat.
In the joy of our shared delight,
Together we'll light up the night.

**Visionaries of the Heart**

We gather like moths to a bright lamp,
Chasing dreams while eating a cold ham.
Laughter erupts like a fizzy soda,
Sparkling moments—an endless moda.

With wild ideas in mismatched socks,
We plan our escape from ticking clocks.
Sugar rush visions swirl like a dance,
In our chaos, we find our chance.

## The Chants of Shared Experience

Under a blanket of cosmic woes,
We wear our quirks like a badge that glows.
In our laughter, reality bends,
Pretzel thoughts shared with silly trends.

Each mishap becomes a classic tale,
Like cats on leashes, we rarely fail.
Our voices blend in melodic cheer,
An orchestra for all who will hear.

## Lighting the Path of Connection

With ice cream sundaes that tower high,
We debate who's the best, you or I?
Spoonfuls of humor, sprinkles of grace,
Illuminating every kooky place.

Through tangled thoughts and gumshoe plans,
We build our empire with silly fans.
Like fireflies dancing on a warm night,
We paint the town in hues of delight.

## Resonance of Compassionate Souls

In the jumble of thoughts like a jigsawed game,
We play off each other, never the same.
Grinning like cats with our tails in the air,
In this grand circus, we banish despair.

With friends who see life through a comic lens,
Witty remarks are our greatest defense.
Together we venture, we rise and we fall,
Crafting a tapestry—funny for all.

**Whispers Beyond the Veil**

Ghostly giggles in the night,
Spooky friends, what a sight!
Casper jokes with ghoulish flair,
They float and laugh without a care.

Haunted halls echo their cheer,
Phantom pranks draw us near.
In shadows deep, we dance and sway,
Who knew dead folks could play?

**The Alchemy of Familiarity**

Mixing laughter like a brew,
Silly stories, old and new.
Potions made from shared delight,
It's a riot, day or night.

Friendship's spark ignites the fun,
Stirring chaos, oh what a run!
Turning moments into gold,
The secrets of our hearts unfold.

## Serenade of Soul-Mates

Two clowns juggling dreams and pies,
In a circus of goofy lies.
Together we dance, fall, and trip,
Fueled by giggles, love, and wit.

Silliness sparks a joyful tune,
Making mischief under the moon.
With every laugh, our spirits soar,
A duet forever, who could ask for more?

## Bonds That Bridge the Silence

A quiet lunch, then boom! A joke,
Our laughter, a conversational smoke.
With a wink and a cheeky grin,
Even silence can be a win!

Teasing tales of days gone by,
With every chuckle, we learn to fly.
Bridges built from shared delight,
Turning quiet into pure dynamite!

## A Symphony in the Silence

When laughter fills the empty air,
We dance like socks that pair with flair.
The whispers of our silly songs,
Echo where the joy belongs.

With every snort and giggle shared,
Our wild tales are never impaired.
We spin around like tops in glee,
In this quiet, we are three.

## **Hands Held in Heartfelt Bonding**

With sticky fingers and a grin,
We share our snacks, and let love in.
Like glue, we stick in every mess,
Together, none could ever guess.

Through mishaps, we find our way,
Like lost socks, we're here to stay.
With silly dances, we unite,
Our laughter paints the world so bright.

## **The Spirit of Together Weaving**

We braid our stories, thread by thread,
With much ado, and books unread.
A tapestry of joy we spin,
With every mishap, we begin.

Through tangled yarns, we find the charm,
Each stitch we make keeps us from harm.
With laughter as our guiding light,
We weave our hearts both day and night.

## **Radiant Ties that Bind Us**

In goofy poses, we unite,
Our pictures capture pure delight.
With sparkly ties and mismatched shoes,
We make the best of all our blues.

Like jellybeans that dance and sway,
We stick together, come what may.
With silly hats, we face the breeze,
Our bond, a treasure, sure to please.

## **Finding Home in Each Other**

We gather round with a goofy grin,
Our jokes like sparks ignite the din.
A pot of laughter, we all dive in,
Together we thrive, and no one can win.

With snacks and tales, we paint the air,
Dancing like socks in a mismatched pair.
A treasure chest of joy we share,
In this quirky tribe, nothing can compare.

## The Warmth of Familiar Strangers

At first, you're odd, just strangers anew,
But before you know it, we're a wild crew.
Each quirk a jewel, each laugh a clue,
Together we shine, in our mismatched shoe.

With silly faces and playful jests,
We conquer the world, at our very best.
In this swirling chaos, we find our rest,
A whimsical bond, truly blessed.

## **A Tapestry of Togetherness**

Threads of humor woven tight,
A tapestry bright, what a silly sight!
Knitted together, we sparkle with light,
In our little circus, everyone's polite.

We spin the yarn, both cheeky and bold,
With stories that shimmer, never old.
In laughter's embrace, we feel the hold,
A patchwork of love, in colors so gold.

## **The Light of Affectionate Souls**

A flicker of joy in the dimmest room,
We dance with the shadows, dispelling the gloom.
With quirks and giggles, we quickly zoom,
Creating bright sparks, like sunflowers in bloom.

The light that we share is silly and loud,
A beacon of warmth, so brilliantly proud.
In our cozy circle, we form our crowd,
With hearts full of laughter, we're joyfully cowed.

## **Threads of Affection in Bloom**

In a garden filled with laughter,
We plant our quirks like seeds,
With every joke, a petal bursts,
And friendship grows with speed.

We water it with funny tales,
And sprinkle in some cheer,
Who knew that silly antics,
Could make the bond so clear?

As we dig up old memories,
With shovels made of fun,
Our hearts become a patchwork,
Stitched together, one by one.

So let's gather 'round the blooms,
With snacks and happy glee,
For in this patch of giggles,
Blooming joy is all we see.

## When Hearts Align Like Stars

Two hearts that dance like comets,
Swaying through the cosmic tease,
With every quip and nudge we share,
We spin the universe with ease.

We chart our course on laughter's map,
Each giggle, a guiding light,
As silly stardust fills the air,
We sail through endless night.

Bumping in the galaxy,
With mess-ups, oh so grand,
We laugh at our own stumbles,
As we float hand in hand.

So here's to cosmic friendships,
That tickle every night,
For in this stellar chaos,
We shine, oh so bright!

## The Pulse of Shared Journeys

On paths where laughter echoes loud,
We wander in silly sync,
With every step, a story blooms,
And joy's the bond, we think.

We trip on puns and punchlines,
As we race through every mile,
Our feet may fumble in the rush,
But our hearts are filled with smiles.

From coffee spills to happy falls,
Each moment's gold, it seems,
We string together witty tales,
And dance in our wild dreams.

So here we are, two wandering souls,
In the rhythm of our ride,
With every chuckle shared, my friend,
We take the world in stride.

## Heartstrings Strummed in Unison

With ukuleles of our laughter,
We tune our lives just right,
Each chord a shared adventure,
That sparkles in the night.

As we strum through ups and downs,
With rhythms quick and bold,
Our friendship sings a silly song,
A melody of gold.

We pluck the strings of memory,
In harmonies so sweet,
With every riff and playful jibe,
We create a joyful beat.

So let's play on, dear buddy,
In this concert of delight,
For when we laugh together,
The world feels so just right.

## **Warmth in Every Word**

A smile that warms the coldest night,
Bringing laughter, pure delight.
With jokes so silly, they touch the heart,
We bond in humor, never to part.

Every word, a golden thread,
Weaving joy, nothing to dread.
Chasing shadows with silly puns,
Together brighter than a hundred suns.

In giggles shared, our spirits soar,
Like birds who dance, forever more.
With every quip, our hearts align,
In this fool's paradise, all's divine.

## The Spirit of Understanding

We glance and nod, no words are needed,
In our cocoon, all worries heeded.
With knowing looks and cheeky grins,
Our banter begins, where laughter spins.

We'll roast each other, just for fun,
In this jesting, we're never done.
A wink, a nudge, a playful tease,
In our circle, we move with ease.

Moments shared, as time flies by,
With every laugh, we touch the sky.
In understanding, we find our place,
Laughing together, a warm embrace.

**Together, We Rise**

In clumsy steps, we find our groove,
With every trip, we laugh and move.
A chorus of chuckles, the sweetest sound,
In this dance of life, together, we're found.

Falling over, oh what a sight,
We rise again, filled with delight.
Like balloons afloat in the bright blue,
Our spirits lift, and our bond renews.

With each misstep, a tale unfolds,
Joking and jiving as life unfolds.
Together we rise, not a care in sight,
In our crazy dance, everything feels right.

## The Dance of Familiarity

Twirling around in a playful spree,
With inside jokes, it's plain to see.
Our hearts beat loud, a joyous tune,
Beneath the sun or the glowing moon.

We trip and laugh, it fuels our fire,
In this dance, we never tire.
Each step brings joy, a comic flair,
Familiar souls in joyful care.

With every shuffle, we break the mold,
In lighthearted jests, our hearts are bold.
Together we twirl, and together we fall,
In the dance of life, we stand tall.

## The Echoes of Shared Dreams

We gathered 'round, all in a mess,
With tales of fumbles, oh what a stress!
Laughter erupted, tea flew in the air,
Our dreams took flight, without a care.

A cat on the counter, a dog on the floor,
While we debated who snored and who swore.
Lost in the giggles, a moment so bright,
The world spun away, oh what a sight.

Spilled secrets and laughter, like confetti on ground,
We danced in our chaos, our joy unbound.
"Wait, was that mine?" I yelled through the haze,
As shared dreams collided in whimsical ways.

With costumes of socks and hats made of cheese,
We set off on journeys, hearts light as peas.
In echoes of laughter, we found common ground,
Our silly adventures, forever renowned.

## **Radiance of Connected Souls**

In a café corner, where we all collide,
Sipping on coffee, nowhere to hide.
Our bright conversation lit up the room,
While pastries danced, chasing away gloom.

A donut debate, icing on top,
Is it too sweet? Oh, just let it plop!
With crumbs on our faces, we ventured to share,
Our radiant moments, none beyond compare.

We laughed until tears streamed down our cheeks,
A group of weirdos, the future looks bleak!
Yet, radiant spirits sparkled so bright,
Together we thrived, all wrongs turned to right.

"Who's wearing those socks?" with a mock frown,
Laughter erupted, it echoed around.
In this splendid chaos, our hearts are so bold,
Connected in fun, worth more than gold.

## Dance of the Understanding Hearts

We twirled through moments, found soil to sow,
With giggles and grins, in one unified flow.
The dance of our thoughts skipped beats, oh so neat,
Like chickens in boots, we couldn't be beat.

A tango of truths, missteps, and quirks,
Each partner united, with plenty of perks.
"Did you step on my toe?" I laughed with a grin,
"Our mishaps are treasures, where fun can begin.

We stumbled on rhythms, a beat so bizarre,
Our friendship held tight, like a jam from afar.
In this wild waltz, we soared like a kite,
Misguided but merry, everything felt right.

As night turned to morning, our spirits did sing,
With hearts intertwined, what joy did we bring!
No dance floor required; we moved through our minds,
In understanding, true laughter we find.

## Harmony in Kindred Echoes

In a room of chaos, where laughter resides,
We harmonized giggles, like musical tides.
Each story was painted with colors so bright,
In the rhythm of friendship, we danced through the night.

"Whose sock is this?" we pondered with glee,
Worn by the dog, but it could be me!
With vibrant discussions and jokes sans regret,
Our echoes like fireworks, we'd never forget.

We shared little secrets, cake crumbs in tow,
While drawing out laughter, it started to flow.
In this quirky harmony, so joyful and bold,
Our tales intertwined, like yarns that we fold.

So raise up your mugs, let the laughter ignite,
In corded connections, we shine oh-so-bright.
With smiles and chuckles, a family we make,
In echoes of joy, our hearts never break.

## The Lanterns of Friendship's Light

In a pub filled with laughter, we raise our drinks,
With stories so wild, you won't believe the stinks.
A cat in a top hat danced across the floor,
And a dog in a bow tie won't bark anymore.

Together we wander through silly mishaps,
Like tripping on words or mistaken maps.
We giggle at chaos, we share all the glee,
In a world full of friends, we're as happy as can be!

The lanterns we carry shine bright on the night,
Filling hearts with warm joy, making spirits take flight.
With jokes and with jests, it's a merry parade,
Friendship's true magic, never to fade!

So raise a toast high, let the laughter ignite,
For together we sparkle like stars in the night.
In this circus of life, we dance with the cheer,
With kin by our side, there's nothing to fear!

## Tapestry of Kindred Journeys

In this wacky world, we weave our own fate,
With threads made of laughter and pastries on plate.
A sock on my dog, I could swear it can sing,
While we plot our next pranks, oh the joy they bring!

Our journeys entwined like a tangle of yarn,
I wore shoes that sparkled, but oh how they'd scorn.
Through mishaps and magic, we stumble and run,
With giggles like fireworks, we shine like the sun!

Each twist in our tale paints a picture so bright,
In the canvas of chaos, we dance and take flight.
From beaches to forests, we leap and we play,
Creating a story that won't go away!

With every wild road that we've traveled with glee,
We paint our own mural, just you wait and see!
Through mishaps and laughter, we always find time,
To treasure this life in its sweet, silly rhyme!

## Beneath the Canopy of Trust

Beneath leafy branches, we gather with cheer,
A picnic of snacks, and oh, what a smear!
With sandwiches flying and ants on the spree,
We laugh until stomachs ache, wild and free.

The fruit of our labor is sticky and bright,
We share all our secrets with furry delight.
A squirrel steals our fries; we give it a shout,
But it scampers away, leaving us with no doubt!

In this quirky haven, trust grows like a vine,
With humor our language, we drink and we dine.
Through failed charades and a game of charades,
We find common ground in the funniest shades.

As the sun sets low, we're wrapped in a glow,
With friendship as strong as our favorite show.
So here's to the laughter, to bonds ever true,
With every wild moment, I'm happy 'cause of you!

## **The Symphony of Loyal Hearts**

In a concert of chaos, we play our own tune,
With pot lids and spoons, our laughter a boon.
A kazoo in my pocket, a drum made of pie,
We orchestrate giggles that soar to the sky!

Each note a remembrance, each tone filled with light,
As we dance through the madness, our hearts feel so right.

With a quirk in our step and a wink in our eye,
We harmonize friendship, no doubts left to pry.

Our symphony mingles like flavors in stew,
With laughter our essence, we craft something new.
From each silly stumble to grand crescendos,
We find joy in mischief, wherever it goes!

So let us keep playing, with humor our guide,
In the symphony of life, let laughter collide.
With friends by our side, there's no need to rehearse,
For every odd moment is a verse in our verse!

## **Connection Beyond the Horizon**

Across the miles, we share a laugh,
Like two old socks in a silly gaffe.
With silly memes that take the cake,
We bond like glue in every quake.

In distant lands, we play our roles,
Sending jokes like bouncing balls.
Distance shrinks when humor's near,
Our chuckles echo, loud and clear.

Through chirps and pings, our spirits soar,
Like ducks in a row, we quack for more.
A virtual hug, a wink, a cheer,
With you, my friend, there's nothing to fear.

So let's keep dancing on this line,
With laughter sweet as aged fine wine.
In the end, it's all a blast,
Connections thrive and friendships last.

## **Lanterns in the Dark**

When shadows creep and fears ignite,
Your jokes are lanterns, shining bright.
We giggle as the night grows long,
In the dark, our hearts belong.

With every pun, we light the way,
Like fireflies dancing at the end of day.
Our laughter weaves a tapestry,
Brightening moments, wild and free.

Though storms may come, and troubles swirl,
We find our joy in a silly twirl.
With every fumble, we share a grudge,
As kindred souls, we'll never budge.

So raise your glass to friendship's spark,
Together we can face the stark.
In our lantern's glow, we'll dance and sing,
In the dark, it's love we bring.

## Kindred Hearts Intertwined

Like tangled wires in a faulty cord,
Our shared mishaps have struck a chord.
With every blunder, our lives align,
Two goofy hearts, forever entwined.

You laugh at my puns, I snort at your style,
Side by side, we make it worthwhile.
In moments of chaos, we share a grin,
Together we lose, together we win.

From dad jokes to tales of woe,
We let our humor steal the show.
Your quirks and laughs I can't resist,
In our friendship, there's no twist.

So here's to us, the misfit pair,
With every quip, we take to air.
In this tapestry of laughs anew,
Side by side, just me and you.

## **Echoes of Unseen Bonds**

Like shadows dancing in the sun,
We laugh so hard, life's just begun.
The world may spin and troubles play,
But your humor brightens up my day.

In whispers shared, our secrets bloom,
With giggles echoing in every room.
Through thick and thin, we share the ride,
With silly faces, we can't hide.

In mundane moments, we find our glee,
Two peas in a pod, just you and me.
With chuckles and snorts, we break the ice,
In this world, there's nothing thrice.

So let's keep laughing, my dear old friend,
With every joke, our hearts will mend.
In unseen bonds, we truly find,
Life is better when we're hilariously combined.

## **A Symphony of Familiar Spirits**

We dance to tunes from yesterday,
In mismatched socks, we sway away.
Laughter bubbles like a soda pop,
We spin until our eyes go plop.

With cookie crumbs upon our face,
We race to find the fastest race.
Each footstep is a joyful cheer,
Our silly games bring friends so near.

Whispers shared beneath the moon,
Plotting pranks to make hearts swoon.
With a wink and a joyful nudge,
We laugh so hard, we'll never budge.

Though time will change, and seasons swap,
Our bond remains—a never-stop.
In every chuckle, every jest,
Together we find joy's sweet nest.

## **Nurtured by Shared Dreams**

In a world where wild dreams take flight,
We ride on clouds, both day and night.
Bouncing ideas like a bouncy ball,
With grand hopes and snacks, we have it all.

Together we plot our next delight,
Baking cookies through the starry night.
Yet somehow, flour flies like snow,
Creating chaos that we love to sow.

We plan adventures with candy maps,
Finding treasures in silly traps.
Each giggle echoes through the trees,
As we chase dreams like buzzing bees.

With voices loud and spirits bright,
We weave through laughter, pure delight.
In each sweet moment, we all gleam,
Bound together by our silly dream.

## **Stories Woven in Kindness**

Once a cat wore a giant hat,
And danced around like a curious brat.
We penned a tale where ducks could fly,
Laughing till tears formed in our eye.

With every word, our silliness grows,
A pirate ship made of marshmallow rows.
Adventures spill from our eager lips,
As we trip over our playful quips.

Every mishap turns to golden lore,
Treasure maps drawn on our kitchen floor.
A ghost who loves to tickle and tease,
Has joined our crew, and it's sure to please.

With kindness wrapped in joyous glee,
We spin our tales, wild and free.
Through laughter, we grow, side by side,
In every story, our hearts collide.

## **Brothers and Sisters of the Soul**

Side by side, we're a funny troupe,
Making mischief in a zany loop.
With sticky fingers and hearts so bold,
Our tales of laughter are pure gold.

Every pillow fight ignites the air,
As we tumble around without a care.
The world is ours, a playground vast,
Where silly moments forever last.

In our circle, there's no room for frowns,
Just goofy hats and mismatched gowns.
With every giggle, we twirl and spin,
Creating chaos as we dive in.

From dawn till dusk, the fun won't cease,
A bond so strong, it's purest peace.
In the laughter that we generate,
We find our joy, oh, isn't it great?

# **Embracing the Spirit of Community**

When neighbors gather for a feast,
The dog steals the chicken, oh what a beast!
Loud laughter echoes, the wine starts to pour,
An impromptu dance goes right out the door.

Cookies in jars, a mysterious blend,
We nibble with joy, never want it to end.
Uncle Joe sings to a misplaced tune,
While Aunt Sue tries to dance under the moon.

Mismatched socks, oh what a sight,
We all laugh as we twirl in delight.
In this mad circus of love and of cheer,
Together we thrive, with no need for fear.

So bring out the games and the popcorn, too,
In this quirky party, there's enough for you!
We raise our glasses, toast our sweet fate,
For who else could bear all this silliness straight?

**In the Company of Light**

A candle flickers, the shadows play,
Making us giggle when things go astray.
With warm hearts laughing, we share the light,
As we bumble through jokes and a game of fright.

Laughter erupts like a fizzing pop,
When Tim drops the snacks—oh! What a flop!
Spilled soda and giggles, a sweet sounding song,
Our bonds growing stronger, where we all belong.

In this cozy nook, it's fun to be free,
Like cats in a box, we pounce with glee.
Embracing the quirks that make us just right,
We dance in the glow, under stars so bright.

So let's fill our cups and toast the night,
In the company of friends, life feels just right.
For amidst all the chaos, we find a way,
To celebrate friendship, come what may!

## Bonds Forged in the Fire of Friendship

We met by the grill, with burgers on high,
As smoke filled the air, and sparks flew to the sky.
Each tale we told was a flavor so bold,
A recipe forged in the tales we hold.

A spontaneous trip with all of our gear,
We lost the way home, but shed not a tear.
Stuck in the mud with our laughter so loud,
Who needs a map when your heart's in a crowd?

We roast marshmallows and share our dreams,
S'mores in hand, we're bursting at seams!
From awkward beginnings to this joyous world,
In friendship's embrace, our flags are unfurled.

As evening wanes, we share one last cheer,
For the bonds we've built, we'll always hold dear.
Through fires and fun, joy's never misplaced,
In this riot of friendship, we're perfectly graced.

## The Language of Unspoken Understanding

A knowing glance, the start of the laugh,
With a single roll of eyes, we split in half.
No need for words, our thoughts drift and dance,
In this silly symphony, we take a chance.

When coffee spills and a friend jumps high,
Together we giggle, not a worry nigh.
Cue random dancing in a public place,
With twirls and spins, we win every race!

We share a silence, an understanding so rare,
As the world goes crazy, we just pull our hair.
With quirky gestures, we break down the walls,
In this language of laughter, love always calls.

So here's to the bonds that need no design,
To laughter that bubbles, and spirits that shine.
In our strange little world, all is well and grand,
With friends by our side, we truly stand planned!

## **Roots That Deepen Together**

We planted seeds for laughter's bloom,
In gardens where the friends consume.
Each joke a wild and quirky sprout,
Together we laugh, there's no doubt.

With roots entwined, we dance and sway,
In muddy boots, come what may.
Our gang's a mix, a colorful stew,
A recipe only friends can brew.

When one slips on the silly pie,
We break out laughing, oh my, oh my!
Through thick and thin, and mirthful blight,
We plant our humor, day and night.

So here's to roots that twist and twine,
In laughter's soil, our spirits shine.
No matter the weather, we'll share a cheer,
With every chuckle, our bond draws near.

## **The Circle of Kindred Hearts**

We gather 'round, a quirky clan,
Sipping tea from a jester's pan.
Each tickle leads to fits of glee,
In our circle, there's room for thee.

One says a pun, then all take flight,
Like butterflies who took a bite.
With every banter, our joy expands,
In this circle, life's in our hands.

Think of a game where no one wins,
Just goofy tales and silly spins.
We laugh till we drop, side-splitting sound,
In this merry band, pure joy is found.

The world may frown and shadows chase,
But in our circle, we find our place.
With hearts aligned in a playful art,
Together we dance, never apart.

## Beyond Words: A Shared Existence

With silent laughs, we share a glance,
In awkward moments, we do our dance.
A wink, a nudge, a gesture so sly,
With no need for words, we reach for the sky.

In the realm of awkwardness, we find our groove,
A shared existence, a silly move.
Each gasp and giggle, a secret exchange,
In the art of being, we never change.

Comedic timing, no script to abide,
In this fantastic world, we take pride.
From foot-in-mouth to snorting loud,
We celebrate life with our funny crowd.

With inside jokes, we paint the air,
In unspoken bonds, we lay our share.
For in every moment, be it quirky or grand,
We laugh through the chaos, hand in hand.

## **The Melody of Affinity**

In harmony's tune, we sing our song,
A mix of chaos where we belong.
With off-key notes and laughter bright,
Our symphony plays into the night.

The beat of friendship, a funky sound,
In this cacophony, joy is found.
With claps and stomps, we get it wrong,
But in our folly, we grow so strong.

A dance-off in the kitchen, wild and free,
With spatulas and spoons, we groove with glee.
Each silly moment, a cherished refrain,
Together we'll laugh through sunshine and rain.

With every high note, every silly fall,
We weave a melody that enthralls us all.
For in this rhythm, our hearts convene,
In the laughter of love, we reign supreme.

## The Mosaic of Connected Journeys

We laugh at the quirks we all share,
Like socks lost in a laundry dare.
With stories tangled in a colorful thread,
We stitch our moments, never misled.

Laughter echoes in our merry troop,
As we trip through life, a clumsy group.
Each step a dance, each misstep a jest,
In our patchwork hearts, we're truly blessed.

Sometimes we fall, sometimes we glide,
Yet side by side, we take it in stride.
A quilt of blunders, a map of delight,
In this wild ride, everything feels right.

So let's toast to the fumbles we make,
Each wipeout a chance for giggles to quake.
With each wacky twist that fate brings our way,
We build our mosaic, come what may.

## **Light Within Shared Shadows**

In the dark, we shine like stars,
With jokes bouncing off like quirky bars.
We fumble in shadows, but don't you fear,
Our laughter lights up even the drear.

At midnight feasts, we raise a toast,
To the goofy moments we cherish the most.
With each silly tale, our spirits ignite,
In the play of shadows, we find our light.

Beneath starlit skies, we wrestle with glee,
As shadows dance with wild jubilee.
In our circle of giggles, we cast all our fears,
Creating a glow that outshines the years.

So let's fumble through life, with a wink and a grin,
Finding the humor in where we've been.
In every shared shadow, a spark we can trace,
Together we twinkle, finding our place.

## The Nest of Mutual Understanding

In our cozy nook, we gather round,
Where laughter's the only rising sound.
With quirks and oddities, we build our nest,
A haven of humor, where we can jest.

Feathers of friendship, a ticklish heap,
With stories that make us giggle and leap.
Each quirky tale wrapped in delight,
In this silly space, everything feels right.

We poke fun at ourselves, it's true,
With silliness brewing in everything we do.
Like birds of a feather, we sing out of tune,
In our happy house, there's always room.

So let's fluff our nest with the quirkiest ways,
In mutual laughter, we brighten our days.
With each peck of joy, we learn and we grow,
In this nest of laughter, we steal the show.

## Warmth in the Circle of Friendship

Around the fire, our stories unfold,
Of daring escapades, both silly and bold.
We roast marshmallows while sharing a grin,
And laugh at our blunders, where we've been.

With each crackle, the warmth finds its way,
Silly antics mark the end of our day.
In this friendly circle, we shed all our pride,
As we giggle together, side by side.

Our quirks are the sparkles that light up the night,
While synchronized eye-rolls give way to delight.
With jokes that cringe and moments that sing,
In this circle of warmth, we celebrate spring.

So here's to us, the weird and the wise,
In laughter we flourish, to everyone's surprise.
Together we skip through the jests that we dart,
With every chuckle, we strengthen our heart.

## The Comfort of Shared Journeys

Two friends with maps all upside down,
   Wandering through a sleepy town.
They laugh at signs that lead them wrong,
   Making memories to last along.

With snacks in tow and jokes to share,
   Driving in circles without a care.
Each wrong turn, a reason to cheer,
   Creating stories that bring us near.

A flat tire leads to a dance in the street,
   Two left feet, but hearts skip a beat.
The laughter echoes, a joyous sound,
   As silly adventures come all around.

So here's to journeys that twist and twine,
   With friends who turn a wrong way just fine.
In every giggle, a treasure we find,
   Unscripted moments, pure and unlined.

## **Nestled in the Arms of Connection**

Two souls collide on a crowded train,
Sharing snacks through the window pane.
With silly faces and goofy grins,
Strangers become where the laughter begins.

A shared umbrella in the pouring rain,
Drenched but laughing, forgetting the strain.
Dancing puddles, splashes so bold,
Kindred spirits in stories told.

They swap their quirks, their dreams, their fears,
With every chuckle, their bond endears.
Late-night chats that turn into snorts,
Friendship forged in the silliest sorts.

So if you find joy in the oddest sights,
Revel in laughter that lights up your nights.
Together we stumble, together we shine,
In the cozy warmth where the twists intertwine.

## The Glow of Kindred Light

Under twinkling stars with a bag of chips,
Sharing secrets with spontaneous quips.
Two mugs of cocoa in fluffy socks,
Creating warmth that happily shocks.

A candle flickers, casting shadows around,
Every giggle, a delightful sound.
With marshmallows flying across the night,
Laughter erupts, igniting the light.

Funny stories take awkward turns,
With each new tale, the bonfire burns.
Ghosts of past blunders come dancing near,
Kindred spirits chase away all fear.

So gather 'round with hearts so bright,
Revel in moments, take flight in delight.
For amidst the glow that we've ignited,
Friendship shines with love ignited.

## **Tides of Togetherness**

Sandy feet and a radio's tune,
Friends creating a festival in June.
With buckets of laughter and waves to dive,
Making memories come alive!

A beach ball bounces with effortless grace,
Raucous cheers show the joy on each face.
Even the seagulls join in the fun,
Sharing their fries, one by one.

Timed with giant splashes and glances askew,
The tide pulls back, revealing the crew.
Sandcastles crumble, but laughter stays,
In the light of friendships that always amaze.

So here's to the tides that bring us near,
Scribbling stories, year after year.
With waves of laughter, we dance with delight,
Together we navigate life's endless night.

## **Souls Dancing in Unity**

We twirl like leaves in a gale,
Laughing at life without fail.
With socks that don't quite match,
And stories that always attach.

A hop, a skip, a quirky dance,
Bonding through every silly chance.
Collecting moments, oh so bright,
Underneath the twinkling light.

Sharing snacks that don't quite blend,
A spicy tale, a trusty friend.
With hiccups of laughter we find,
Our silly jigs leave woes behind.

In the chaos, we find our groove,
Every blunder helps us move.
Together, we defy the norm,
With giggles our hearts keep warm.

## Embracing the Ties That Bind

Two peas in a pod, they say,
We stumble through life in our way.
Our plans, like jigsaw bits, fit,
As we share the craziest wit.

With mismatched shoes on our feet,
We dance at the strangest beat.
Baking cookies that flop and fall,
Yet always we answer the call.

Chasing down the ice cream truck,
Splattered in ketchup is just our luck.
With charm that's anything but bland,
We paint the world hand in hand.

When life throws us curves to greet,
We laugh and admit our defeat.
In this hodgepodge we call a crew,
Crazy fun shines brightly and true.

## Celestial Friendships

Stars twinkle in our nightly chats,
As we share cookies with no spats.
Galaxies in our silly schemes,
Creating laughter like swirling beams.

We orbit like planets in deft spins,
Chasing rainbows, we always win.
With snacks that fly into the sky,
Our giggles make comets go by.

With faces painted in clever ways,
We share our secrets, our fun-filled days.
Gravity can't bind our zest,
In this friendship, we are blessed.

Through the universe, our jokes soar,
Painting spaces with laughter galore.
Together we jest, and thus we thrive,
In this cosmic joy, we feel alive.

## Harmony in the Silence

In comfy corners, we share a glance,
While sipping tea, we do a dance.
No words needed when hearts align,
In silence, our laughter twines.

A wink exchanged, our secret clue,
We roll our eyes, just me and you.
Tickles and nudges feeling so sly,
In silent moments, our souls fly high.

Baked goods burn; our laughter ignites,
In quiet battles, we win the fights.
With silly faces that say it all,
Our bond will never let us fall.

So here's to the joy found within,
In silent chuckles, our stories spin.
With just a glance, a shared delight,
In the hush of friendship, everything's bright.

## **In the Garden of Shared Spirits**

In a garden where laughter grows,
Friends gather round, striking silly poses.
With pie fights and glee, we dance in sun,
In this patch of joy, we're all just one.

A gnome wears a hat, much too big,
While daisies gossip, giving a jig.
The daisies gossip, the pine trees sway,
In this wild garden, we laugh all day.

Worms tell jokes, but it's hard to hear,
As frogs croak out puns, bringing good cheer.
We share in secrets, stories, and cake,
In this blooming space, we're wide awake.

As sunset beckons, we sit on the lawn,
Exchanging our dreams 'til the light is gone.
With twinkling stars, our hearts intertwine,
In this garden of spirits, it's always fine.

## Kindred Spirits in the Quiet

In the little nook, all cozy and warm,
We sip our tea and plot the next charm.
With giggles so soft, we whisper and share,
These moments so sweet, beyond compare.

Our shadows dance lightly, shadows we cast,
Poking fun at the things of the past.
Teacups clink softly, and we both smile,
Life's little nuances make it worthwhile.

A cat on the windowsill joins the spree,
With a yawn and a stretch, 'Oh, do look at me!'
In this sacred space, mere laughter will soar,
Each chuckle a treasure, we always want more.

The clock gently ticks, but time feels at bay,
As we swap our tales, in a quirky ballet.
With hearts in alignment, we sit side by side,
In the peaceful quiet, our spirits abide.

## **The Bridge Between Hearts**

A bridge of giggles, spans across time,
Built of silly stories and silly rhyme.
We leap with joy, through puddles of cheer,
Each step on this path, draws us more near.

The wind whispers secrets, we promise to keep,
As we dance through the air, like two silly sheep.
With clumsy steps taken, together we hum,
Creating a melody, blissfully dumb.

Through the heart of the bridge, we share some pie,
With whipped cream mustaches, oh my, oh my!
Hand in hand we stumble, laughing out loud,
In each other's presence, we're blissfully proud.

As we reach the other side, hearts open wide,
Friends forever, through the ebbing tide.
With chuckles that echo, we'll always roam,
On this bridge of laughter, we've found our home.

## Echoes of Unconditional Affection

In a room filled with giggles, we set out to play,
Crafting inside jokes, that brighten our day.
The echoes of laughter bounce off the walls,
While we burn the cookies—oh, the baking fails!

With high-fives and cheers, we chase down the news,
Sharing all the gossip, and silly reviews.
We roll on the floor, in fits of delight,
Through this whirlwind of fun, we stay up all night.

The clock's laughing too, as we race against time,
With cups overflowing, and some chocolate slime.
Through each crazy moment, we feel more alive,
Our hearts knit together, let's joyfully dive!

In this wild circus, we're the stars of the show,
With echoes of friendship that loudly will grow.
Through mishaps and laughter, our spirits unite,
In this joyful adventure, everything feels right.

## **The Grains of Shared Time**

When laughter tumbles down like sand,
We sift through moments, hand in hand.
With each tick of the clock, so fine,
We gather grains of joy, divine.

In silly hats, we dance and sway,
Sharing tales that lead us astray.
The world spins madly, but here we stay,
In giggles and gaffes, we find our way.

Our memories are like jellybeans,
Sweet and sticky, filled with dreams.
Oh, the shenanigans we've seen,
In our little realm, we reign supreme!

So let's raise a toast to our grand parade,
To the clumsy leaps and the pranks we've played.
In this circus of life, we're not afraid,
For in our merry chaos, love's displayed.

## Heartbeats in Synchrony

With every heartbeat, a skip and hop,
We find a rhythm, never stop.
In the symphony of friendship, we sing,
Even off-key, we find our bling.

Bouncing jokes like balls in the air,
With each punchline, we become a pair.
Syncopated laughter's our favorite beat,
Our quirky steps move to a funny seat.

We share snacks like two playful kids,
Trading candy bars and giggling bids.
In our oddities, bright colors ignite,
Our hearts beat loudly, a joyous sight.

As we march in unison, side by side,
The quirks and quirks become our pride.
In this wild dance of glee, we stride,
Together, forever, a joyful ride.

## **Whispers of Heartfelt Kinship**

In whispered secrets behind closed doors,
Our giggles escape like playful roars.
With every silly prank that we devise,
We plot our capers under the skies.

Daydreams flutter like colorful kites,
In the canvas of our fanciful nights.
From tickle fights to late-night chats,
We're two grown kids in vibrant hats.

With every mishap, we find our role,
In the theater of life, we're on a stroll.
A comedy act where we take the stage,
With lines so funny, we laugh with rage.

In the warmth of laughter that binds our soul,
We embrace the quirkiness that makes us whole.
So here's to the whispers, the fun, the kin,
In this world of ours, may the laughter begin!

## **Threads of Shared Souls**

We stitch our lives with laughter's thread,
Each yarn a tale that's widely spread.
In mismatched colors, we find our style,
With a wink and a nudge, we laugh all the while.

Our friends are buttons, quirky and bright,
Sewn together in the fabric of light.
In marvelous patterns, we twirl and spin,
With threads of nonsense, the fun begins.

From fabric flops to fashion faux pas,
We strut our stuff, never a flaw.
In our patchwork quilt of joy, hold tight,
With each silly stitch, we unite our might.

So let's embrace our patch of delight,
In this tapestry of love, we ignite.
With laughter as our thread, we sew the day,
In the loom of friendship, we find our way.

## In the Circle of Shared Wishes

We gather 'round with silly dreams,
Each wish a burst of laughter beams.
One hopes for shoes that tie themselves,
Another wishes for dancing elves.

With pies that fly and socks that sing,
We spin our hopes on wobbly string.
If wishes were horses, we'd all ride high,
Galloping under a pastel sky.

A cat that talks in rhyme and jest,
A squirrel that wears a tiny vest.
With every giggle, our hearts collide,
In our goofy world, we take pride.

So let's trade dreams, let's share a grin,
With every chuckle, the magic begins.
In this circle of wishes, wild and free,
We find the joy in absurdity.

## A Sanctuary of Kindred Laughter

In our haven of hilarious cheer,
The jokes are bright, the laughter near.
With ticklish toes and squeaky shoes,
We share a world of quirky views.

A comfort found in silly schemes,
Like wearing hats made of whipped creams.
A dance-off with our pet goldfish,
Fulfills a most ridiculous wish.

Together we spill secrets galore,
Like which of us can snore the more.
In fits of giggles, we light our days,
In this sanctuary, we toast our ways.

Our laughter echoes, a joyful sound,
In every corner, happiness found.
Let's keep this laughter, let's hold it tight,
In our little world, everything feels right.

**Voices of Unseen Allies**

We speak in whispers, unseen yet near,
Mischief makers, we hold dear.
With bubbles that tickle and pies that fly,
We plot our fun beneath the sky.

Invisible support in every jest,
Our funny stories never rest.
With silly hats and rubber ducks,
We're a band of goofballs, just our luck!

When storms roll in, we dance and spin,
With every jab, we let the fun begin.
Our mighty laughter a shield so clear,
Against the gloom, we persevere.

In the tapestry of goofy delight,
Our unseen voices shine so bright.
Together we triumph, hilarity our prize,
In this comical world, we're wise.

## The Garden of Empathic Hues

In our garden where giggles bloom,
With every chuckle, we chase the gloom.
Laughter sprouts like daisies tall,
Amongst the joy, we shall not fall.

Petals of humor in colors bright,
With tickling vines, we take flight.
A water fountain that drips with grace,
Squirrels darting in a wild race.

Our friendships flourish, a cheerful sight,
In this garden of mirth, hearts ignite.
Every guffaw a seed we sow,
In the soil of kindness, we grow.

So come and wander, take a stroll,
In our playful patch, happiness is whole.
Where the sun shines bright and laughter reigns,
We find our joy in each other's veins.

## **Beneath the Same Stars**

Beneath the same stars we gather round,
Telling old tales that are quite profound.
With laughter that tickles and quirks that delight,
We're a silly bunch in the soft moonlight.

We dance like the wind with two left feet,
Tripping and tumbling, oh what a treat!
Our voices combine in a chorus so loud,
Making the crickets feel more than proud.

A toast to the mishaps, the bumbles, the blunders,
To friendship that blooms beneath all our wonders.
We'll giggle through nights where the jokes barely land,
Creating our stories, an oddball band.

So here's to the stars that wink with a grin,
To moments we share where the laughter begins.
With joy in our hearts, and pie on our face,
Let's cherish the chaos, the charming embrace.

# **Unraveling the Threads of Belonging**

We gather and stitch from a fabric so bright,
With patterns of laughter in the dim twilight.
Each thread tells a story, so awkwardly spun,
In the tapestry woven, an errant pun.

Like mismatched socks on our feet in the night,
We embrace all the quirks, nothing feels right.
Our jests may unravel like old, frayed clothes,
Yet together we shine, no one ever knows.

We tie all our dreams with a ribbon of glee,
In this craft of our lives, so humorously free.
Each snort and each giggle a verse in our song,
Reminding us all that we truly belong.

So raise up your glasses, here's to our crew!
To friendships that flourish in everything new.
With laughter as glue, we are stronger than fate,
A patchwork of joy that we all celebrate.

## **Reflections of Togetherness**

A mirror we hold, with cracks here and there,
Reflects all our quirks that we boldly share.
With giggles and snickers, our tales come alive,
A bond made of chaos, together we thrive.

We play peekaboo with the lives that we lead,
Hiding in laughter, or just being silly.
With jokes that misfire or tales that just flop,
In this jovial whirl, we cannot just stop.

Like snippets of movies we'd never rehearse,
We bloom in absurdity, sharing a verse.
Each moment a snapshot, our laughter the light,
In this gallery of life, our spirits unite.

So here we stand, a glorified mess,
With humor and heart that we all can confess.
Let's raise our toast to this jolly parade,
In the reflections we find, all the fun that we've made.

## When Hearts Align

When hearts align like spaghetti and sauce,
We tangle in laughter and sometimes in loss.
Our mishaps are treasures that shimmer and shine,
In this goofy charade, we know we're just fine.

With parfaits of stories layered so thick,
We scoop up the moments, each bite a quick pick.
With puns that escape like a cat on the run,
We chase after laughter, we're never outdone.

Through joy and through chaos, we sprinkle our spice,
Our moments together, both lovely and nice.
So here's to the times that feel oddly sublime,
In the rhythm of friendship, there's no need for rhyme.

So laugh with abandon and dance with a friend,
Our hearts beat together, a bond without end.
In the symphony woven by laughter and cheer,
When we gather as one, it's the best time of year.

## The Strength of Embraced Differences

We're a puzzle, odd-shaped and bright,
Each piece fitting, just right.
You've got polka dots; I wear stripes,
In this quirky blend, there's no gripes.

Laughter dances, curls like our hair,
You trip on words; I trip on air.
Together we create such a scene,
Comedy gold, a sweet routine.

When you fall flat, I'll be your cheer,
With dorky jokes, we'll conquer fear.
Our differences bloom, like flowers in sun,
Embracing the weird is oh-so-fun!

So here's to us, the awkward brigade,
In this circus life, we're unafraid.
United we stand, a jolly parade,
With laughter and love, our bond is made.

## **Threads of Connection**

A web of quirks, we weave each day,
Stitching together in the oddest way.
You snort when you laugh, I laugh at your snorts,
Our threads of joy form funny reports.

With tangled tales and shared mistakes,
We're weaving memories, drinking milk shakes.
Your jokes may flop; mine fall flat too,
Yet here we are, just me and you.

Each rewind brings echoes of glee,
In our fabric of life, want to join me for tea?
Laughter's our glue; it's sticky and sweet,
In a patchwork of friendships, we find our beat.

So here's to our threads, both bright and frayed,
In this colorful cloth, let's never fade.
Crazy and silly, our bond's so unique,
Together forever, with laughter we sneak.

## The Essence of True Kinship

We're like two peas in a quirky pod,
Stumbling through life, it's something to laud.
You're the tofu to my spicy dish,
Together, we're full of a wacky wish.

In laughter's embrace, we find our tune,
You make me dance like a silly cartoon.
Our friendship's a recipe, a dash and pinch,
With a sprinkle of chaos, it's sure to clinch.

When the world's a bore, we shake it up,
With wild antics, we fill our cup.
In the circus of life, we're the stars of the show,
With each giggle, we continue to glow.

So let's toast to kinship, goofy and true,
In our wild journey, there's always room for two.
With jokes and laughter as our guiding lights,
Our essence shines on through glorious nights.

# Companions in the Whispering Wind

Two odd socks on the line, we sway,
Whispering secrets, come what may.
You talk to trees; I chat with clouds,
In our whimsical world, we stand proud.

With breezy smiles and gusty cheer,
We chase the wind and the butterflies near.
You tell the worst jokes, I laugh the loudest,
Together we fly, never the shroudest.

Through gusts and gales, we stumble and spring,
Dancing 'round the sun, we laugh and sing.
In every bump, a story unfolds,
With every breath, the laughter beholds.

So here's to the winds that carry our song,
In this funny bond, where we all belong.
Through whispers of joy, we find our way,
Companions in nonsense, come what may.

**Shared Laughter**

We chuckle at the pizza place,
Sharing crusts and sauce with grace.
All our jokes, a silly spree,
Laughter rolls like waves at sea.

With every pun, our eyes grow wide,
Like kids we giggle, side by side.
A joke once told, now legends grow,
In this laughter, joy will flow.

Our antics often lead to cheer,
Like clowns who dance, no trace of fear.
Tickled bones and snorts abound,
In this circus, love is found.

So here's to fun, our silly dreams,
The friendship forged in laughter's beams.
With every chuckle, we ignite,
A spark of joy, a shared delight.

## **Shared Tears**

A mishap witnessed, chocolate spilled,
On white shirts, laughter's filled.
We wipe our eyes, so full of glee,
In tears there's joy, as friends we see.

When life feels heavy, and clouds hang low,
Our giggles rise, like a warm glow.
With every tear, a tale we weave,
Each misadventure, a laugh we believe.

So grab the tissues, we'll have a show,
Where laughter dances, and sorrows go.
In puddles of tears, we find our way,
Transforming heartache into play.

Together we face this wild ride,
In every tear, there's joy inside.
Through shared moments, we will learn,
That laughter's spark will always burn.

**The Embrace Beyond the Physical**

We don't need warm hugs to show,
Our bond's a dance; look how we glow!
Like shadows side by side we play,
In our own world, we drift away.

With secret looks and knowing grins,
Our special language is where it begins.
No need for touch; our spirits meet,
In every laugh, we feel complete.

Through silly dances and whispered jest,
Our connection grows, it's simply the best.
While hugs are nice, there's more to share,
In every chuckle, we're always there.

So join our crew, it's pure delight,
In this friendship, everything feels right.
Beyond the physical, we intertwine,
In joyous spirits, our souls align.

## **A Canvas of Kindred Connections**

With bright colors, our stories blend,
On this canvas, laughter won't end.
We paint with jokes, a vibrant hue,
In each stroke, our bond shines through.

Splatters of fun, and splotches of glee,
Our canvas grows with each memory.
Brushes dipped in happiness, we strive,
Creating art where we feel alive.

When things go wrong, we just make a scene,
Splattering paint, oh what a dream!
In this playful mess, we find our way,
A masterpiece of delight, come what may.

So join this dance, let's color the air,
With laughter and smiles, it's beyond compare.
Our laughter will echo, our spirits fly,
In this canvas of warmth, together we lie.

## **Glimmers of Mutual Light**

Like fireflies dancing under the stars,
We light up the night, no need for cars.
Our laughter twinkles, bright and free,
A constellation of fun, just you and me.

Each glimmer brings warmth, like summer night,
In our little world, everything feels right.
When shadows loom, we shine so bright,
Together we spark, like stars in flight.

With giggles that glow, we chase away gloom,
In our playful chase, joy starts to bloom.
Through every bump, we light the way,
In this glowing bond, we safely stay.

So here's to the giggles that lead us on,
In our friendship, the magic's never gone.
With every spark, our spirits ignite,
In laughter's embrace, we find our light.

## **Journeys of Interwoven Paths**

Two friends set out with snacks in tow,
One brought cookies, the other, a crow.
They laughed at the bird, it stole their lunch,
But they welcomed it in with a quirky hunch.

Through forests and rivers, they treaded with glee,
Chasing odd creatures, and shouting with spree.
A squirrel stole a sock, they swore it was fate,
Now fashionably matched, they dance with their mate.

Navigating through detours, they plotted their way,
Turning mishaps to tales of marvelous play.
They tripped on a rock, and fell in a stream,
Laughed 'til they cried, each bobbling gleam.

At journey's end, with hearts all aglow,
They vowed to return, wherever they'd go.
With stories to share and laughter so loud,
They cherished each moment, standing so proud.

## The Chorus of Mutual Love

A pair of old pals sang tunes they thought grand,
Off-key in the park, both clapping their hands.
They tried to be serious but burst out with glee,
Chorus turned chaos, like bees in a spree.

With ukuleles in tow, they jammed on a whim,
Dancing like ducks, then falling limb by limb.
Neighbors all chuckled, their faces turned bright,
"What's this ruckus? Is there a duck fight?"

One wore a hat that was way too too tight,
The other just twirled, what a humorous sight!
Their voices mixed up, confusion in tune,
Yet laughter soared high, like a warm afternoon.

In this silly choir, their hearts intertwined,
Music and friendship, a harmony blind.
With each silly mishap, their spirits took flight,
Together as one, a jubilant sight.

## **Gentle Hearts, Strong Connections**


A cat and a dog, the strangest of pairs,
Sharing a blanket, exchanging their stares.
They plotted and schemed over snacks and a toy,
Each snatched treats from mouths, oh what joy!

In gardens they tumbled, like leaves in the breeze,
Chasing a butterfly, tripping with ease.
Their owners just watched, baffled by the scene,
"Is this paws or just nonsense? Who knows what they mean!"

At dusk, they both yawned and curled on the floor,
Trading warm purrs and playful encore.
The dog snored so loud it rumbled the night,
While the cat played the tune with a flick of delight.

With friendship like theirs, the world felt so right,
Two souls in the same, each making a light.
In their quirky adventures, so simple, so sweet,
They showed everyone life is a marvelous treat.

## Beyond the Veil of Solitude

A cloak of silliness wrapped 'round their days,
Two curious friends with whimsical ways.
They danced in the rain, all drenched to their shoes,
Contemplating cupcakes and gathering views.

"Is that a cloud or the sky's mooing cow?"
One giggled, while the other thought, "Wow!"
Imagining dragons that slipped through the mist,
They made silly plans that were hard to resist.

In the forest, they found enchanted old shoes,
"Let's wear them!" they squealed, "Let's share all our views!"
They pranced through the trees, atop the soft ground,
Echoes of laughter, the most beautiful sound.

In their odd little world, they banished all strife,
While hopping through puddles, they danced through their life.
With friends by your side, no one's ever alone,
In the land of the quirky, together they've grown.

Milton Keynes UK
Ingram Content Group UK Ltd.
UKHW021938121124
451129UK00007B/133

9 789916 943342